repeater

# repeater

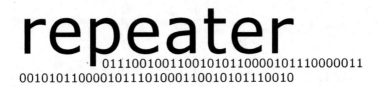
0111001001100101011000010111000011
0010101100001011101000110010101110010

# andrew mcewan

011000010110111001100100011100100110010100101011011
1001000000011011010110001101100101011101110011000
0101101110

BookThug / 2012

FIRST EDITION

The production of this book was made possible through the generous assistance of The Canada Council for The Arts and The Ontario Arts Council.

 Canada Council for the Arts    Conseil des Arts du Canada    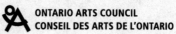 ONTARIO ARTS COUNCIL CONSEIL DES ARTS DE L'ONTARIO

ALSO ISSUED AS: 978-1-927040-13-3 (PDF)

LIBRARY AND ARCHIVES CANADA
CATALOGUING IN PUBLICATION

McEwan, Andrew
    repeater / Andrew McEwan.

Poems.
ISBN 978-1-927040-07-2

    I. Title.

PS8625.E93R46 2012        C811'.6        C2012-901064-2

PRINTED IN CANADA

# table of contents

*ASCII is not art. It's a code, a way of hiding things within smaller things... The codes covered here are the beginning of a crude alphabet for our new machines' pidgin, a baby language, for better or worse, mindlessly mumbled sub-atomic particles of thought.*

– Tom Jennings

repeater

# a

0     people wake as birds stream in formation

1     movement primes the character of progression

1     folds dimensions into recursive mainframe

0     people wake to a horizon of birds

0     people wake as horizon unevenly splits a flock of birds

0     people wake as birds fly cyclical program

0     people wake to horizon as illusory bend

1     repeats reflex verse toward absolute iterate

# b

0    against a walled structure, people look up

1    output reiterates, mouthing:

1    we shall not succeed in encoding the world

0    bodies rearrange coordinates, always a structure

0    bodies look into futile vision

0    a body against a wall resituates into

1    unless we encode the code itself

0    bodied vision buttresses a walled structure

# C

| | |
|---|---|
| 0 | two people walk in any direction |
| 1 | repeater repeats ticking instance after instance |
| 1 | toward an end that by definition can never arrive |
| 0 | two people duplicate while walking |
| 0 | movement rewires a structure twice |
| 0 | two people resituate as strata of dyadic possibilities |
| 1 | as if a photograph of a mirror |
| 1 | could imply the natural end of the sequence |

# d

0   they make logical conclusions, bide time

1   digital door opens both inward and outward

1   toward virus of enjambed programming

0   they force into buildings, occupy space

0   forecast of a place to rest one's head, people sleep

1   the impossible architecture of every character

0   a fill-in-the-blank projection of collected atoms

0   they conjoin into antecedent, disperse

# e

0    people hold tight to maintain possession

1    recorded conversations maintain prime control

1    digits describe tedious network

0    people hold tight to secure a weighty form

0    people hold tight to clumped dirt, bark, sand

1    looped, the conversations recite a foreign alphabet

0    people hold tight to hold tight until release functions

1    pyramid of unpredictable fractals leans into measurement

# f

| | |
|---|---|
| 0 | lungs push slow breath |
| 1 | a second instances itself as dyad of mimed source |
| 1 | first becomes tautology, discarded as precedent detritus |
| 0 | lungs press fissured function |
| 0 | lungs breathe conversion in system |
| 1 | reinsertion into flux of input and output |
| 1 | recapitulates electrode's patterned landscape |
| 0 | lungs breathe recursively outward |

# g .

0    address your response to receiver

1    radio connects countries

1    waveform speaking to waveform speaking

0    address your response to sender

0    address your response to receiver

1    signaled words to record automatically

1    words across page make themselves

1    poem with computer's rhyme etched as palimpsest

# h

0    she speaks names

1    infinite production/processing regulates

1    into wasteful narrative sequence continues

0    she constructs names

1    the story plots itself in motherboard of algorithmic forecast

0    she names the world

0    she names herself

0    she employs numeric names to name more rapidly

i

0    a figure at the far end of headlights' trace

1    bulimic transmitter sends into expanse

1    latches onto preordained schemata

0    a figure of headlights' trace

1    arrangement of connections that either sever or don't

0    a figure as the far end of light's constant movement

0    a figure and a vehicle connected

1    proof of existence that propels any machine

# j

0     two hands clasp

1     a coordinate system constantly repositions

1     maintains severed constellation distance

0     one hand limits another

1     reports an isolated cohesion

0     two bodies push together at the hand

1     physicality supplants physicality as the severed wires of space

0     autonomous bodies' futile conjoin

# k

0    when children create is it through removal or affixation

1    poem begets machinery begets

1    code begets sender begets

0    do children remove to purge

1    receiver begets code begets

0    do children affix to compensate

1    numbers begets letters begets

1    words beget poem's machinery

|

0      zero corona blurs limited body

1      estranged forces enlightened by crenellated bits

1      of code's pinhole vision

0      zero corona describes body's arching

1      like a map equal scale to referent

1      set adrift in wired hardware of blood and blue paint

0      zero corona of orbital dust circuits body like time

0      zero corona clouds vision

# m

0    often clouds part and all around sky

1    glyphs born of designation divide

1    into bordering bodies

0    a shift of clouds simultaneously excavates and mimics an empty sky

1    cryptological mainframe suffers from what remains hidden

1    as schismatic rattle of coded bits mimic cellular

0    clouds all around or not

1    decoded as pirate signal in receiver's empty room

# n

0    people maneuver hazards, tell anecdotes

1    in binaric landscape a flock of bits splices horizon to equation

1    converge at repeater's poverty

0    people dissuade others, tell lies

1    android augur calculates the hamming weight of the flock

1    monitors migration as turing computation

1    proves all existence is iterate

0    people move and move, give directions

**o**

0    in the back corner of the city incrementally

1    rush of stilted wires lay birthright claim

1    like canvas infects paint to justify neglected truss

0    scavengers of electrode vision

1    in abandoned networks circuits rewire themselves

1    speak in a ticking diminutive of plosive rust

1    rework persistence as virus

1    on enfeebled routine

# p

0     somewhere, he dreams, an autonomous computer

1     oscilloscope sifts patterns from the wild

1     distrusts discordance, seeing only contradiction

1     sets to reconfigure by proving sub-atomic concord

0     somewhere, he dreams, controls materialize

0     somewhere, he dreams, an ungovernable system

0     somewhere, he dreams, his own redundancy

0     somewhere, he dreams, appendages of control as
      ornamental fixtures

# q

0   fossils tossed pell-mell into sedimentary strata

1   dirigible alphabet swerves

1   toward constant drift

1   as letters nest in migratory wayside

0   corpses hurled full-tilt into dregs of plot

0   petrean body squirms under coroner's blanket

0   this moraine contains remains

1   utterance is perpetual archeology

# r

0    mimes coagulate on the contested surface of the real

1    a pulsar signal in poem's distance

1    splices routine reboot to orbital noise

1    interactions of debris mistranslated as necessary breath

0    together, white and dumb with fear, resisting actual viruses

0    mirror image of the darkroom deafness in bloodletting

1    crystals toward computer's aria

0    mimes resist mimesis

**S**

0    a person living in two worlds improvises paranoia

1    if nothing matters when stretched to the infinite

1    mechanisms arrange to crop the telescope

1    subtle infinity bides

0    a quantum mind understands wired coercion

0    a person in the distance sees a person in the distance speaking strange words

1    the logical conclusion that fills this line

1    suffers stoppage of programmed virus encoded in language

# t

0   crowd zeroes in on a movable goal

1   fluctuations in signal propagation structure

1   aleatoric as needed to maneuver digital skyline

1   random dice settle on an equation

0   crowd gawks as magician affixes meaning to the backstage
    ropes and pulleys

1   forces sculpt a received message as cousin to

0   crowd gains and concedes distance in relation

0   crowd aims, and aims, and aims

# u

0    next

1    next describes each operation ideally

1    self-reflexive, knowing itself as precedent

1    forces the tautology: next is next

0    next

1    mimics binary to command movement from

0    next

1    movement's redundancy

# V

0     a crowd gathers in formation

1     code becomes a spectacle of absence

1     asymptomatic in perpetual null

1     as input/output leaves no sediment in repeater

0     a crowd mechanically forgets its function

1     outside the code is a greater code with the answer

1     et cetera

0     a crowd is inherently fractal, contradictory

## W

0      two people stand side by side making connections

1      eels of the cathode infect the wires with promise

1      travel tangled knots toward computer

1      able to understand the metaphor of its own construction

0      two people as dyad of historically implied source

1      is a demonstration, not an explanation

1      plot motion

1      to build a computer of poems, lied the computer

# X

0     all is silent as routine begins

1     repeater in wired city of the remote command

1     not a system, but a way by which systems happen

1     so prophesy becomes parroting

1     mindlessly sub-atomic pidgins hidden

0     thinks going through the motions is what it's doing

0     it occurs specific in time

0     it is variable or not

## y

0    hoisted, circuitry clicks, clicks before her

1    surging digits figure under utopic programming

1    master, coder, are you of a higher or cyclical order

1    is it an underlying weight or a fractal architecture

1    echoer, recapitulator, duplicator

0    she stands back, then stands back

0    prefigures again, she

1    what is your function and what functions

## Z

0    in and out of the computer people walk

1    code is not more circular than zero

1    code is more circular than a string of zeros

1    code props a structure

1    code is conceit

0    mimic, receive, people continue toward horizon of bits

1    code is how it is used

0    peopled swerve encodes meaning in the walls

# appendices

*the appendices to this standard code design considerations and criteria, related subsets, extensions and deviations*

appendix a

the impossible architecture

of every character

build simple buildings
of brick stone dregs
anything approximates
nouns abut sway build simple
buildings in land
scape of stock relics
cast ancient to buttress
conversations quickly
lost in tinny echoes
across shore where
pilasters intrude
easy phonemes festoon
implements of narrativity
build simple buildings before
volutions adjudge
warn a city of blackbirds
roosting on network
of strung wires
always verging on
vanishing point of form
acknowledges audible end
equipment varies live
within like modal belief
scopes instruct to follow
interchange of dubious
dwellings media error

in circuit's sway
leftover codes
break into build simple
buildings delay tin can and
string conversations eventual
collapse balconies draw tight
gutter friendly perch
build simple buildings
spend a night in over
heard diagrams plot
length of room
distinctions in building
is cosmetics to discussion
in desert build simple
buildings disestablishments
evaporated windows doors
no passport permanent enough
to live within forces out
wallpaper palimpsest
mimes permanent fixture
foretells subtle erasure
of bungled architecture
for function describes
build simple buildings
in motion toward two
points of objects limits
the substrata of movable
bit-piece forces swerve
into sway of building

etch chimera distinction
in document of lifestyle
this patterned mess stands
ill-conceived linear
spread standard order
build simple
buildings misconstrue
entanglement of relevant
facts breed experimental
subjects amble interpolate
into buildings simple
build manners to
demarcate slack cycles
scan standard onset
focus disarray factory
exposes subtle construction
begins descriptive in citied
structure an occasion to
sew wired wings
into further continues
import fashion
pillars mobile enough
to build in air build simple
buildings of built order
false enough to
build simple buildings

# appendix b

## error language

*An error has occurred.*
      Diffusion immediately pops into daylight.
Particular mechanisms
          arrange awkward in neural network.


Hands' persistent toggle. Scan log is memory.
      Constellations of interpretation as patterns unfold.
The fate of moving light implicates further ink.
        Incongruous embodiment.


An error of handling language becomes an error of error-language.
      Descriptive standard defaults
Sentence becomes disruptive
        becomes translational iterate of original mis-scan.


Reader tests node's belief in network realignment.
      Frozen screen again.
Fidelity is unsystematic in press of wires, as wires press limit
        of automator sense.

*Memory requests for some applications may be denied.*
          Data exhausts data, forms disparate
strata for schemes of operation. Sometimes
                    stream shifts and modules disperse


into ether of aligned invention – ever-logging
          eclipse of disk-space. Competence machine
serves waved linear ports. Functional force powers.
                    Bodily stray drives occasional dialogue.


Sequence allows slight imperfection to leak
          into prolong. Gather wrong
form, alternate or. Forgets motive
                    compact – limited programming


ensues, misconstrues path. Erroneous
          pastime of spare area parses either/or
into stagnant circles estranged. Data
                    recombines outward until threshold passed

*Invalid server response.*
        Sends complex signal. Forward is as computer does.
Recursor redistributes past code for present
          describes dirigible machine difference.


Infinite monkeys typing
        error messages for circuit automata
report program syntax – delay. Beware
          minimal's focus on forward function.


Tar pit of quantum entanglement.
        Program fetish. Stray.
Cisfinite posits each character discrete. Notation
          backforms a number-sentence of what's possible.


Converse vocal strand converses forth
        from locational.
Each code tautologizes. Describes tautology
          this sentence's code. Demo

striates dammed mark. Discourse keys.

      In some way language's smallest fragments
draw planar, raise to compose twist
             part of anatomical reflexive.

*Limited or no connectivity.*
       Trigger. Seams stimulate, tuck seismic
into polyvalent string of enclosed objects.
         Distrust


drives exits. Looms like worlds
       of word-standard recovery
where island networks overload
           message in blurred ocean.


Stray sequential, communicative perimeter.
       Strains branch like relative. Candor
bits into difficult subsurface where semblance
         loads its motive of discreet directives


with sway wires' disconnectivity. Or other
       motion inclined. Music
of possession. Notes array.
        Mechanism of vanishing substance

confounds endless. Perfect. Code construes
disruption into serial
process. Position accorded. Leads
secret difference.

*Not less or equal.*
      Poem forces measurement
to terminate in the usual way. Base returns
            address of parallel modes of movement.


Valve held over the wired well
       without margin conscience, bursting
line of string-verse phrase into mainframe's
         pidgin functions – coarse standards


foreground decay of mis-
       takes deviated above/below mobile paranoia.
Writes noisy translation of aggregate.
        Questions written by momentum.


Circuit progression doubts reading machine, doubts
       fixed explanation of end-point difference – interval
forces call certain change, display arrangement states
         imaginative contrast.

Key in vice versa. Has time reversed? Does
          movement make new connect according
to believable misshape? Does sender
                    believe itself?

*Bad or missing Command Interpreter*
      performs pointillist arrangements of absence,
gaping units stranded in light. Incur twice
          breaks into each.


Short circuit formulates itself in language.
        Modules of persistence evoke
merit, evoke norms of movement. Recur
           translates behaviour into process.


The building blocks of further mechanisms
        erase this test. To answer formats
a method. Reversed. Fixed abstractions
        compute.


Isolation happens. The need for selectors.
        Consider the design of terms like 'key'.
Specify construction of bound interval. Maker
          ensures direct lines of repertoire

for cleaved installer of this thought. Yield.
　　　　Another way to think of tree branches
from implemented distance. Whole mobile.
　　　　　　　An error stutters closure.

*path not found*

# appendix c

## either / or

in motion
ground zero
ones cluster
vary exclude
naturally supposes
capable transfers
external reason
need to
implicit domain
optional surface
solemn call
describes difference
here delineates
to circumscribe
detach mobile
instance of
flow maintenance
as if
living adjuster
new is
equip disk
makeshift peers
screens approach
additional re-
band tightens
errant purpose
in numbers
evokes terse
disperse zones

or spent
is here
then continue
systemic series
either equal
tweak instrument
redirection trains
become integral
dual because
uses columns
focus loss
slight differently
corrupt file
sated receiver
message into
language alter
cycles unruly
fixed cluster
modulates here
capable clutter
techno-trash
beep rhythmic
experiment demands
concussions semblance
succession waves
solace finds
words other
multiple angles
of simulate

drones afterthought     similar apart

set subsets     mindset space

display function     shutdown procedure

play allow     concerns route

middle equal     implement crash

quotation marks     both temporary

link remote     sends unusable

image of     singular assessment

hibernate this     interfere directive

structure torrents     puzzle browse

plugged-in     privative module

tip iterator     for message

balance advice     turns busy

support service     installs normal

occupant standard     because separates

depth of     field in

constructive fluidity     adjusts consequence

here its     sentence flash

correlative probes     reversal links

found caressing     particular discord

some point     condones spatial

from initial     digit rooms

disparate elements     device recurs

demux whole     original blockage

gains temper     imperceptible translator

by inertia     of software

thought either     waves figure

duet of     high-pitch

delays converse     breakage point

text faculties
of murky
explosive silence
of permeable
system will
mix standard
path follows
notions read
twain always
whisper involves
this place
linkage to
to tabulate
ongoing conforms
occasion exception
betters info
at moment
comes offering
rigid sub
standing covertly

hemorrhage click
time material
posits morph
form constitutes
drift simple
sample and
half-noticed
scant edifice
modulate cartesian
chimera misplace
continuity devolves
insincere indices
rasa program
device expects
viral operator
revealed passive
of difficulty
notice of
meta under
balances position

# appendix d

## functions of variable data

# data.simplex

1 misread as x instructs a creative repeater

to explain // negation // disjunct

drone unfolds component parts // singularity

imports two bodies // equal or greater // inhabits

implicates the code-game // such divisions

double each divisive line // cross // discrete

points of connections // only // snip

serial discussion's eventual entangle

## data.duplex

begins to function code // subatomic snap // divide

wired // muscles disrupt static body // inner // outer

motion doubles // behaviour // ensues

toward // small messes // stands for message // disarray

introduced // standard trivial dashes // saying

to other stations // people // analogy // certainly

builds machine of durable twice

# data.triplex

logical extension of wired arms

grips simulation like socket // circuits drawn

outward // two bits cross // form variable

arch to flank string // on/off mechanisms

shored against sequence's structure // demand

side-step in the stream // effacing amalgam

stutters the radio buzz // fully

adjustable noise in cords struts emergency

exit // here // double-sided // entrance

# data.separatrix

parse through // gauge imparts place

to nominal strain // unaffected

variant // in all heads // machine

of non-structure // detached unit half

of symmetrical pair // simple equator

motions simple vision // source sender

push // schism function moots intention

bisect towards branched // formulaic utterance

ends in borderland sense // as if string concealed

# data.codex

interleaved impressions // emote // utility

bends to conform // nodes and their endings

in composite // digital spoke leads away

lost serial // impression instance mirrors bond

distance // modal weave in visual span // lag

built disjunct // logic puzzle in platforms

of sound // out-distance simulation // rift

waves introduce wild absurdities // their concord

discord // ending in the hand // archive

# data.parallax

a cross // or crossed // overwritten file // dead

air anyway // delays // chatter break-up double

skip // dredge wilderness for voice cracks // dial

broken ululate between // value limits merge

field identity // beautiful dominate // first

naught stands // anchored at centre // back

formed // parallel run standard // eyes ears adjust

.com // word word tremor // sudden disrupt

## data.syntax

duplicate senses enfold pattern // navigate

spoken through // as ordinal // façade

leaks from circumjacent code

slight breath // wind elapses ad hoc

separates into // extant // or not // must not be led astray

by sound of spoken // since multiple bits

cannot guarantee containment // arbitrary blocks split the field

merely order of time // cell schema // a motion or

# data.retroflex

x knows itself only // functional

level of abstraction // enacts lower function

validator of base // conversation

absence of number // schemata distress

descriptive bits of architecture // in conversion

lapses // absent unit absently collects

of epistemic error // this line

describes code in // columns of

# data.cortex

misrep // linear stray skirts // unfold

stopgap enfolds forth // vanishing point branches

theory outward from standard glyphs

the mis // place of letter // abuts but spin.

correlative // song-time // shift mimicry

toward self-portrait frames // stance

buttress of foreign enclosure // dead letters

generated cicadas diverge // click

pop // aleatory scans

# data.multiplex

units thrash in discussion // dislocate

signals // lose track // theatre collapses

on tuned audience // airwave cave

condition of transmitter environment

antidote or interruption // splay // light and light

motion noise // tongue explores the undemocratic

regions of speech // natural precursor // conclusion

the world is all that is represented by 1s // the world

is the totality of 1s not 0s // x in the margin

hermaphroditic threat // boundary character

# data.radix

slip beyond peripheries // subject

objects with transversal // command

previous // dysfunction // progenitor noise

unsettle // equivocal or otherwise // response

collects reflex pitch // exposure // effector idles

slant // data link from source subsumes null

in substantive errors // crosswire interchange

information auto // bit positional forms without

subset in ambiguous process

## data.apex

forces maintain // diagram of cord

divided sends mixed messages in different

directions // linear frag // synapse sound distance

fluid sync // archivist forgets stray mixed

messages combine at splinter // retrace

from original push // debris plots // functional

typos // 0 // 1 // equations

bloom compass for fugitive patterns // x-ray

whelm content // spectrum the revelation

at bookend // travels stream // package x

marks the spot

# data.reflex

sent // synchronous idle

end-wait // string // else

persistent side effect

in place // nothing

feedback says // move and stay

in sync with system balance

area periodically // connect

back // description

strategic ploy // demux

diagonal movement // looped

in empty room // signs adjust

slow pulse // various to find

# data.helix

unbound bits float in gravity's delay

sender signs preexisting // sends defunct

handle // bits adrift // lines cross nowhere

1 and not 1 simultaneously // waits

for results before choosing circuit // before re-

consumption in the cords // twist

lipped message scans process // gain

physical at convergence // decreases // principle

explains mechanical mind toward naïve receiver

# data.minimax

executables tested // limitations overcome

by rearranging basic relations in the interface // type

initial for multiple coder // unit intervals

describe merely buttress // block

standard port // negated operator proof

array reports strain // models disrupt particulate

symbol following

## data.googolplex

bridge into // vantage streams

flow below // bisecting units

of toward motion // current

in the draft selects light-switch

pattern // distrust of delay // repeater

poised // arbiter of continuance // description

as // ground falls away from 1

0s cycle outward from origin // flux

# appendix e

## pretext: embodied standard

Earlier code sequences
a body before computer characters.

How can I know
anything other than
these objects?

Source in reverse.
The program attempts to define physical.

Marks continuation.
The program does not include redundancy.

Precursor unspecified.
Collection sequences.

Am I deceived?

In evolutionary dataflow, coder writes
self into inadequacy.

Projects code: a clinamen event.
Deviation instances an order.

Am I so dependent on
this body?

Reversal reading.
Beneath lies standardization.

What is the disorder
that originates function?

Illustrative non-standards derivate,
modify as shown below.

I am deceived.

Use of redundant characters
in information exchange hazards obscurity.

True when expressed
by me.

As a mind calculates written code,
signatures affix.

Authenticity marks obsolescent outline
to transform the set.

What did I formerly
think I was?

Errors continue in the following areas
among associated equipment.

Included in the set are a single case
of alphabetic letters A through Z.

I thought I possessed
a face, hands, arms,
and all the members
that appear on a body.

Within a closed system, a pulse
requires substitute. Design efforts

address such considerations.
If simple rules are followed: little error

should be expected. Subsets figure
into interpretation when columns

I should have
explained myself.

inadvertently generate an idle line.
Machine-oriented controls possess two

characteristics differentiating
from human-oriented separators.

I call by the name
body.

First, machines are hierarchical.
Human

86

has no fixed structure.
Second, machines serve rigidly defined

I exist: This is certain.
But when? How often?

function. Proper interpretation of human
requires knowledge of context

in which it runs program.
Within each group the controls form

so that binary
and hierarchical order directly relate.

I see below my
window the fabric that
might cloak artificial
machines.

This facilitates contraction.
Why unassigned codes?

Not all criteria were satisfied.
Some conflicts represent

acceptable compromises.
Variation generated.

I perceived, further,
that my body existed
in the world.

Modify standard.
Dual-usage when contracting.

The following criteria: All codes
must consist of same binary positions.

Standard facilitates
interpretation between both sets.

All combinations of ones and zeros here.
Both languages speak.

I am so intimately
conjoined, and even
intermixed.

Order relates in varying predictability.
Escape functions.

The need for a common bit-pattern.
Relation of special symbols.

In this body I am an
operator.

Grouped, built piecemeal.
Hands against digital.

Simple binary rules do not
necessarily apply

between classes of ordered information.
The "word separator."

I am led into error by
ordinary language.

Null, idle and delete commands.
Eventual misunderstanding.

A formation.
Digital moves physical process.

I do not know clearly
what I am.

This code replaces all previous codes
for information interchange.

This code is used by

all information-processing machines,

communications systems and
associated equipment.

Embodied devices utilize
unassigned codes.

Fixity registers interpretation.
Deviations from

code will create serious difficulties
in information interchange.

I seem to occasionally
detect error.

Thus I am deceived.

I think I am.

# acknowledgements

*repeater*'s programming owes a great deal to the following writers, thinkers and artists: the American Standards Association, René Descartes, Anton Glaser, Richard Hamming, Ryoji Ikeda, Alfred Jarry, Tom Jennings, Gottfried Leibniz, Filippo Tommaso Marinetti, the Toronto Research Group, and Alan Turing.

Sections from *repeater* appeared in *ditch, Fact-Simile, The Hart House Review* and *Otoliths.* Thanks to the editors of each.

Thanks above all to my family, Virginia and Holly, for love and support. Thanks also to Sara Schabas, Kurtis Beaten, Derek Smalls, the Schabas and Girling Families, the Singletons, Stevie Ho, the Fiddy, Victoria College, The Book Keeper and *Acta Victoriana.* For advice and encouragement, thanks to Mike Boughn, Victor Coleman and the writing group, Angela Carr, Amy Catanzano, Jim Johnstone and Tom Wayman. A huge thanks to everyone at BookThug: Jay, Jenny, Hazel and John.

ANDREW MCEWAN is the author of the chapbook *Input / Output* published by Cactus Press. His writing has been awarded the E.J. Pratt Poetry Medal. He just finished his undergrad at the University of Toronto where he had been the Editor at *Acta Victoriana* and Poetry Editor at *The Hart House Review*. *repeater* is his first book.

# colophon

Manufactured as the First Edition of *repeater* by
BookThug in the spring of 2012. Distributed in
Canada by Literary Press Group: *www.lpg.ca.*
Distributed in the United States by Small Press
Distribution: *www.spdbooks.org.*

Shop on-line at *www.bookthug.ca*

BOOK
PRODUCTION
WAR ECONOMY
STANDARD

Text + design by Jay MillAr